Cars

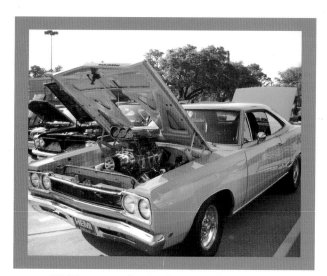

Written and photographed by
Donna L. Cuevas Roeder

This is a red car.

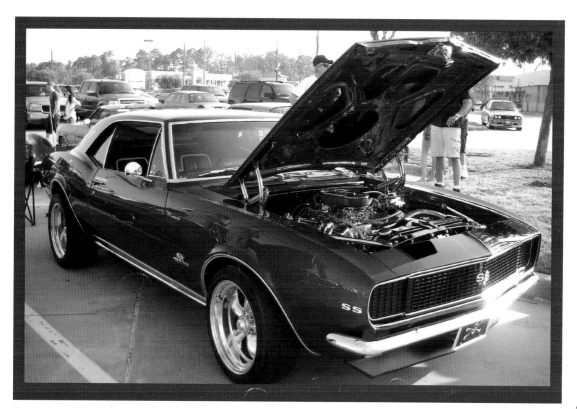

This is a blue car.

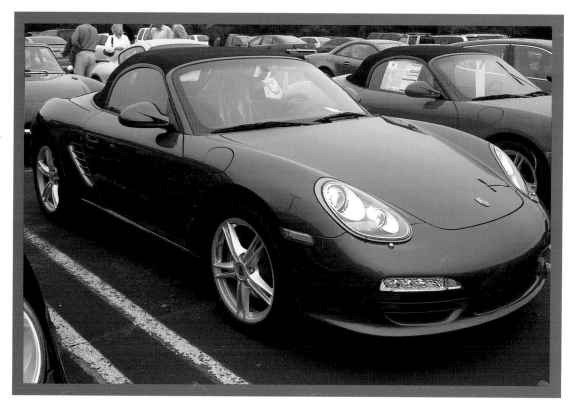

4

This is a green car.

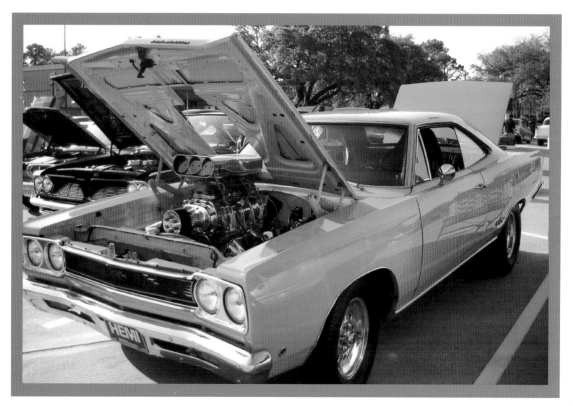

This is an orange car.

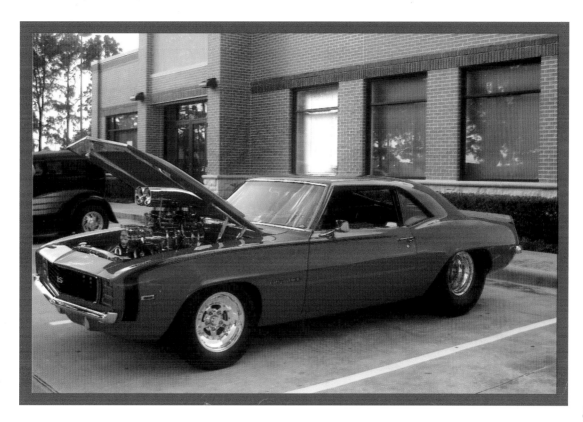

8

This is a purple car.

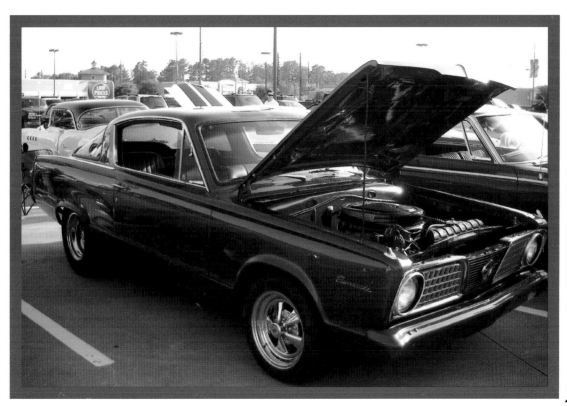

This is a grey car.

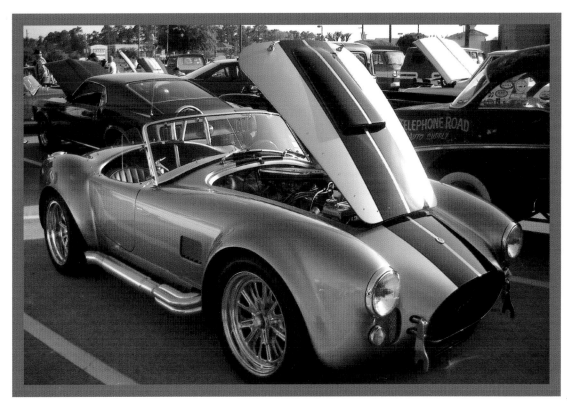

This is a black car.